The Lady in the Wheelchair

*21 Daily Lessons
To A Changed Heart*

Tami L. Sanders

The Lady in the Wheelchair

Copyright © 2015 Tami L. Sanders

All rights reserved.

ISBN-10: 1508404755
ISBN-13: 978-1508404750

The lyrics to the hymn *Count Your Blessings* referenced on page 60 were written by Johnson Oatman Jr. in 1897. The music was written in 1897 by Edwin O. Excell. Copyright, Public Domain.

Lyrics and music to the song *Change My Heart, O God* referenced in this book on pages 73 and 74 were written by singer / songwriter Eddie Espinosa. Copyright 1982 by Mercy/Vineyard Publishing, admin. in North America by Music Services o/b/o Vineyard Music USA.

Unless otherwise noted all scriptures are taken from the Holy Bible, New International Version (NIV). Copyright 1973, 1978 and 1984 by International Bible Society.

Specifically, all scriptures in this book are taken from the NIV Thinline Reference Bible. Copyright 2005, published by The Zondervan Corporation, Grand Rapids, MI USA 49530

Kim,

Always remember

God is with you!

Nami

Tami L Sanders

DEDICATION

This book is dedicated to Linda - my ICU "roommate", my confidante, my caregiver, my dear friend, my mom. Thank you for staying by my side, caring for me, crying with me, praying for me, loving me unconditionally. Thanks for being my cheerleader! I love you Mom.

ENDORSEMENTS

Mark Ivey, Senior Pastor
Christ Alive Church, Newton NC

"Inspired insight comes at special times in our lives, not only to help us but bless others as well. Tami Sanders has written an intuitive, perceptive, thoughtful and sensitive work about real life that not only tells the stories but asks important questions that go beyond the surface to search and answer the deepest questions of who we really are. You will not only enjoy reading this book but grow in your relationship with a living God who so longs to connect with us every day."

"As Tami's pastor, I see honesty from the highs and lows of someone who writes with a transparency that only experiences of life can bring. Open up your heart; this one is a keeper!"

John Fichtner, Senior Pastor
Liberty Church, Marietta GA

"Tami Sanders is one of the most vibrant, alive, cheerful people you would ever want to meet. During the years she served as our church administrator, Tami was truly loved by everyone who knew her. She was a bit of a workaholic simply because she had so much energy and such a zeal to help people. Tami overflows with love for everyone and lights up the room every time she walks in."

"As you will read in this book, Tami's love, joy and zeal come from a very deep place of faith that has been tried by fire. She is one of the pure lights for Jesus that will shine on earth and in heaven. This book will inspire you to walk more closely with our Lord."

Anthony and Margaret Sowemimo, Co-Pastors/Founders
Harvestland International Christian Center, Kennesaw GA
Chosen Remnant Christian Ministries, Powder Springs, GA

"We have known Tami Sanders for many years. We have seen her walk by faith with a cheerful heart, even in difficult circumstances. God is our Healer and Redeemer. This book will encourage you. Whatever you are battling, you will find encouragement in this book."

Tami L Sanders

CONTENTS

ACKNOWLEDGMENTS

My heart will always be full of love for those that walked this
road most closely with me. For the sacrificial care you gave
me and your living testimony of God's love and mercy,
I thank my God for you.
Philippians 1:3

Tami L. Sanders

ABOUT THE BOOK

This is a story of one woman's tragedy and triumph when faced with a condition called Guillain-Barre Syndrome. The author's true story unfolds through a series of 21 short stories followed by 21 daily lessons leading to a changed heart. You may first find yourself caught up in her unbelievable story of struggle, moving quickly through her journey with GBS, before you are able to go back and delve into the daily lessons. *That's ok.* Her journey to a changed heart will become your journey too.

As you read this true story, you may think to yourself *"I don't need a heart change."* **This book is for you**. Or you may be thinking *"I've already had a heart change."* **This book is for you too!** Take this courageous journey with the author and get ready for your own heart to be changed.

When My World Changed

Tami L. Sanders

Lesson 1

WHO ARE YOU?

WHO ARE YOU??   As I looked at her, that's all I could say. I felt I should know her but I didn't recognize her. What first made such an impression was actually the little girl. Blond hair cascading halfway down her back, she was one of those children you noticed right away simply because of her outward beauty. She was about 4 years old and should have been filled with the joys of childhood. Yet, her eyes held strength and determination far beyond her years.

The child was with a man pushing a woman in a wheelchair and a tall handsome boy about a year older. Obviously her family.   They stayed close together as they made their way through the throng of people waiting in line for the show. Others were loud, laughing and talking as they waited for the doors to open, but not the little family. They were silent, merely whispering to each other if they said anything at all. The man slowly pushed the wheelchair carrying his wife, weaving through the crowd. The boy walked in front of the woman in the chair, like he was protecting her. The little girl walked beside the woman, keeping her hand in the woman's or on the arm of the chair. *Is she afraid she will lose her in the crowd?*

Then the man stopped and whispered something in the girl's ear. The little girl grabbed the handles of the chair from him and began to push forward. She seemed to use every ounce of strength her little body could muster as she pushed the lady in the chair. People watched the beautiful child in awe as she maneuvered the chair through the crowd. Most people either turned away to avoid eye contact or stared in disbelief as this tiny little girl pushed and pulled on the chair. Softly I heard her say, *"Excuse me. Excuse me please."* I went with them into the restroom.

As they passed the mirror, I got a better look at the woman's face. The right side of her face hung mostly limp like she'd had a stroke. Her mouth drooped on one side, giving the appearance of someone much older. Her hair was dull and lifeless, as if no one had known how to make it better. As I watched her in that chair, the woman's frail appearance made it clear she HAD to be there. Her eyes held a deep sadness and more than a bit of worry. Her hands and fingers, drawn and weak, were of no help in pushing herself. The little girl stayed by her mother's side, helping with every need, trying to block the opening to the door in an attempt to maintain her mother's dignity. Everyone noticed the woman could barely transfer herself from the chair to the toilet. *Who is she?* And what happened to her?

I couldn't help but wonder what had turned such a young woman with a beautiful family into this lifeless portrait of an old lady. As I looked at her in the mirror, she looked back – straight into my eyes. I immediately turned away. It was almost painful to look at her. But I seemed to be drawn back to her eyes – those haunted, sad eyes, filled with the memories of the monster that had stolen her youth and that of her children. As I stared into those pain-filled eyes, I thought to myself, *"I **know** I know you. What happened to you?"* And then she began to relive her story.

Lesson 1: How do you view others?

When I looked in the mirror at this woman that day, I saw someone who was helpless, feeble, filled with pain, broken. I saw no hope and no rescue in sight. She was just someone who had been struck by a tragedy and was now stuck in a wheelchair.

Isn't that what we do sometimes? We look at someone who seems to have less than us – or more than us – and we make a quick assessment.   Maybe we feel pity for them because of what we see. Or maybe we feel envy for what appears to be great success. Knowing only in part, how often do we walk away with only a portion of the real picture? I'm sure sometimes I totally miss the truth in my narrow view.

Wouldn't it be wonderful if someone who sees the whole picture could just fill in the blanks for us? We can have many questions answered if we ask the right person the right questions. It's easier to see things clearly if you can look through the eyes of the person who knows all the answers.

"If any of you lacks wisdom, he should ask God who gives generously to all without finding fault, and it will be given to him."   *James 1:5*

Lesson 2

A CHARMED LIFE

I've known for most of my life that God sees the big picture. We see only in part. The Bible even tells us that. *("Now we see but a poor reflection as in a mirror; then we shall see face to face." 1 Corinthians 13:12)* But there's a big difference in knowing something to be true, and actually experiencing that truth.

Many would say I've led a charmed life. Grew up with both parents. Christian parents. In a Christian home. A sister. A brother. No abuse. No major health crisis. Parents not only loved each other, they actually LIKED each other. Best friends with my sis. Loved my baby brother. My life was perfect.

Well, of course it wasn't *really* perfect. We had stuff to deal with too. My parents had divorced when I was about 5 years old. I have a few memories of my parents arguing and my sister crying. I seemed to earn the title of "the strong one" during that time. That name stuck with me and always made me laugh inside. Kinda funny that everyone thought I was strong just because I didn't show my emotions. I felt all the same things my sister felt but I kept them behind the curtain like the wizard in oz. I had hoped I could maintain that charade throughout my life but the truth was soon to be revealed.

After a year, my precious parents were remarried and my fairytale romance with love and life continued. My parents made life and love look easy. They walked together, strong in faith and family, never appearing to be plagued with the struggles or crises of others. Little did I know at the time the hours they spent on their knees in prayer, trusting God for miracles in crises that I had not even noticed before.

After high school and my soft attempt at college, my fairy tale life continued. Moved to Atlanta – my dream city. Got a fun job traveling. Became roomies again with my bff, my sweet sis. Then married at 23. A Godly man. Tall, good-looking. Life was perfect.

Well, maybe not *quite* perfect...we had our stuff. Pastoring was tough. Money was tight. We made poor financial decisions. Lost a house. A car. Miscarried our first pregnancy. That was devastating!! Thought I'd never stop crying. But we made it through - Had two beautiful kids. A handsome baby boy then a beautiful baby girl, of course. The perfect family. The perfect life.

When people told me about their "stuff", I would politely nod and say something meaningful, like *"Oh my goodness. I'm so sorry."* But truly, I had no clue WHAT they were talking about! Up to this point in my life, I really thought that no matter what happened, *"I can do all things through Christ who strengthens me"* – with emphasis on the "I" and "me". I believed that when I ran out of strength, God was refilling my tank so I could go on. I had absolutely no idea even what the word *empathy* meant, much less a personal understanding of it. In my mind, I would think *"Poor darling, she really needs to get over that!"* or *"I guess he just doesn't have enough faith"*. I know, **clueless!!**

So, when I woke up that Sunday in late April 1999 with tingling in my fingers and feet, I had NO idea what I was about to face.

Lesson 2: The Good Life

She had the world by the tail. Perfect life. An all American family. Great parents. Happy family life. Beautiful kids. We would look at her and think she's living the dream, right?

Many times we look at outward circumstances – looks, money, job, relationships – and we rate the success of someone's life based on what we see. Often don't we rate ourselves using the same scale? We compare ourselves – even rank ourselves – to others. How often do we put others and ourselves in a box based on this "life score"? There is a *true* scale that provides a more sound assessment of our life. It's simple really.

"The Lord does not look at the things man looks at. Man looks at the outward appearance, but the Lord looks at the heart."   *1 Samuel 16:17*

When we place ourselves and others on that scale, we are equally evaluated. You could say that it's at that point, and only then, that we can *really* see each other clearly.

Lesson 3

JUMPING HURDLES

We had been prepping our home to sell – priming and painting, using all sorts of cleaners inside the house and weed killers in the back yard. I'd been buried in a sea of chemicals for three weeks. Looking back, I remember having a headache for much of those weeks but didn't really think much about it. *Just stress.*

That tingling was weird though. Felt like my hands and fingers were trying to go to sleep. I kept shaking them. *Geez, wake up for crying out loud!* Then, I thought, what's up with my feet? Must be the new tennis shoes I'd bought. Wore them all day yesterday. Probably too tight. Have to remember to loosen those laces.

Monday arrived and brought with it a new friend, numbness. Started in my fingers, hands, toes, and feet and worked its way right up into my forearms and calves. Now this is getting a bit strange, I thought. Told a friend. Probably a pinched nerve, she said. Makes sense. So, I went to her doctor.

Oh, did I mention before that I was SO healthy I didn't even HAVE a doctor?! You know those forms that request the name of your personal physician? I would always list either my OB/GYN (because I had given birth) or my orthopedic (knee surgery – high school tennis injury). Or sometimes when I really felt like bragging, I would simply put "n/a" on that line.

Here I go to the doctor – my friend's doctor.

Migraines.

You said what?!

Yes, ma'am. You're having migraines.

Do you realize you're hyperventilating?

I'M WHAT?

Yes, ma'am. You're probably breathing erratically due to the pain of the migraines. This is causing your oxygen and carbon dioxide levels to be out of balance. And THAT is causing the tingling and numbness.

Hmph!

I sat on the table speechless. Well, it did make sense. Some sense at least. So I took my muscle relaxant and pain killer home and figured I'd jumped one more of life's hurdles.

Hmmm. Not quite.

Lesson 3: What happens when the hurdle's too high?

How many times have you just been minding your own business, running the race, staying in your lane, when all of a sudden you trip over something totally unexpected? You didn't even see it so there was no way to avoid it. Just slammed headlong into something you were not prepared for and fell flat on your face!

Hurdles in life can be so many things. Family crises. Illness. Money. Job. We plan so well, yet it's still not enough. As the saying goes, "Mama said there'd be days like this!" And she was right. Whether you believe in an all-knowing, all-powerful Creator named God or whether you think we all just got here by happenchance, I'm sure you will agree, we ALL have days when we hit the pavement of life. So what do *you* do?

For me, the answer is simple. **Turn to God.** *Really??* *Simple?* I said SIMPLE. Not easy! We know we will have stuff to deal with, some expected and some unexpected. In Psalm 46: 1, David wrote, *"God is our refuge and strength, an ever present help in trouble."* David had his share of trouble. Chased and tormented by the king he would succeed. His own son turned on him and tried to have him killed. David knew he needed God's help.

So, what's *our* problem?

The hard part for us is we've begun to believe we are self-sufficient and don't need God. We have so much knowledge at our fingertips, we actually believe we can manage this life with no outside help. *So, how's that working for you?*

15

Maybe the next time we find ourselves face down on the pavement of life or stuck in the mud of a situation, we should ask God for help, like David did. Then we too will be able to say, *"I waited patiently for the Lord; He turned to me and heard my cry. He lifted me out of the slimy pit, out of the mud and mire; He set my feet on a rock and gave me a firm place to stand."*   Psalm 40:1-2

Lesson 4

PUT IT ON THE SHELF

There are certain days we never forget. Graduation.
Your wedding day. The birth of a child. And the day
you wake up and are numb to the waist, every breath
taking a concentrated effort. The last Tuesday of April
1999. That was the day. The day my life changed
forever. For the better.

Now if you know anything about Guillain-Barre
Syndrome, you just said, *"What?! The BETTER?!"* Stay
with me and I will get to the "better" part.

That morning, I looked at my husband and said,
"Something is bad wrong!! I can't feel my legs! I can't breathe!!"
Normally calm and steady, my husband said, *"What
should I do?"* The only thing I could think of in the
midst of the situation was *"CALL MY MOM!"* Of
course. My wonderful mom.

My parents had been in ministry for most of my life.
They'd seen it all. They would KNOW what to do.

Getting the facts from my husband, mom told him to
sit tight. She would call right back. Mom called the
neurological hospital in Atlanta and received
instructions to get me to the nearest ER. Within
minutes, I was in the ER of a small rural hospital on the

east side of Atlanta.

By the grace of God, the doctor who was on shift that morning had seen Guillain-Barre before. One case. In 25 years. As I said, by the grace of God. The doc immediately ordered a spinal tap. If you haven't had one, pray you never need one. Worse than knee surgery *and* child birth but apparently one of the primary ways to diagnose Guillain-Barre Syndrome. And then the *real* fun began.

As the doctor began explaining to us what having Guillain-Barre may entail, I remember thinking *"Am I going to DIE?!"* I heard him say things like paralysis, numbness, permanent nerve damage, wheelchair bound, ventilator, feeding tube…. *WAIT!! WHAT?! You said WHAT?*

My babies were 4 and 5 – I could NOT be wheelchair bound. Could definitely NOT be on a feeding tube. And yet, all I could think of is *"Am I going to DIE?"* Gotta put that on the shelf.

Yes, *The Shelf.* I'd always been able to do that before. You know those people that seem to never, ever be phased or rattled by ANYTHING?? Well, I'm one of *those* people. Those people get in a major car accident and look around at the destruction and chaos and glibly say, *"Well, at least no one got killed!"* Or their sister comes back in from class, with dirt and mud all over her, blood running down her leg showing evidence of a very nasty meeting with the concrete, and that person says, *"Well at least your hair held up!"* Yeah, THOSE people! Never rattled by life's chaos.

Well, we DO get rattled. We just don't show it. We put that thing on the shelf of our mind to deal with LATER. When we are totally by ourselves and can fall apart by ourselves – like in the shower or the car or wherever – we take that thing off the shelf, process it, scream, cry, and even yell about it. And then, we're good! We come back into YOUR world and walk out another day in that *"I'm SO in control of my life"* picture.

Well, let me just tell you, THIS was NOT one of those days!! This was a day when you can't even pick that thing up to get it ON the shelf! It's too big and way too scary. I was – for the first time in my life – totally OUT OF CONTROL. Of everything.

Lesson 4: I THINK I CAN, I KNOW I CAN...

Remember that childhood story about the little engine that could? He would climb that huge mountain repeating, *"I think I can. I think I can. I think I can."* Then, when he made it to the top – which of course, he did – he would loudly proclaim, *"I KNOW I can. I KNOW I can!!"* all the way to the bottom.

Wouldn't it be nice if we could face every uncertainty with that kind of fearless resolve? Never waver. Never doubt. Just an unwavering confidence that we WOULD make it over that mountain.

It's obvious as I'm reading this woman's story that up to this point in her life, she had been able to walk with that level of confidence. "I KNOW I CAN!" The only problem was she had never really faced a mountain too big for her to climb unassisted. A life of small successes had given her a false sense of security in her own abilities. In her own strength. The day she realized that she was no longer in control and no longer able to regain control was actually the best day of her life. She just didn't know it yet.

The apostle Paul wrote of a thorn in his flesh. Three times he asked God to take it away. Instead God told Paul, *"My grace is sufficient for you, for my power is made perfect in weakness."* 2 Corinthians 12: 7-9

Paul continued by declaring that he would gladly brag about his weaknesses so that the power of Christ would rest on him. Never a more memorable statement was made than when Paul said, *"For when I am weak, then I am strong."* 2 Corinthians 12:10

It doesn't seem like Paul was using the world's standards of strength and weakness to make these declarations. Paul knew that only when he reached a place of humility and powerlessness could God move the mountains in his life. Paul served an all-powerful God. The God that Paul wrote of and followed is the same God that we can relinquish control to today. Hebrews 13:8

Let's see what this woman does when she loses control...

Lesson 5

GUINEA PIG

For the next 19 days, all I could do was lie on my back while everyone on earth, it seemed, looked at me, checked me, poked, pricked and prodded me. I couldn't feed myself. Or toilet myself. Or bathe myself. I couldn't even keep my mouth shut to keep the food in. It would be spooned in and run right back out. The spinal tap was only the beginning of my days as a human guinea pig.

The spinal tap confirmed the diagnosis of Guillain-Barre Syndrome, an auto-immune disorder that compromises your entire neurological system while shutting down all of those systems that normally function on their own – like all of your internal organs!! Upon diagnosis, I was immediately placed in ICU and connected to various life-sustaining and monitoring devices, heart, lungs, circulation. Every opening on my body had something connected and was either beeping or pumping and inflating at will.

By the end of that first day, my mom had moved into my room for the duration. The staff brought her in a bed and placed it right next to mine. Looking back, that should have been a red-flag to the seriousness of my condition. It wasn't until later that I would make the connection.

My husband brought a great gift – music. He brought in our small stereo with a barrage of worship cds, encouraging us to play worship songs 24/7. So mom and I played Christian music 24 hours a day in that ICU unit. Those songs proved to be a blessing straight from God. Nurses and other staff began to "stop by" on their breaks, just to see me AND hear the music. Mom and I got attached to this one song. We had no idea what the words were because it was just the music, no lyrics. It had such a peaceful quality to it that we listened to it every night when we went to sleep. We would let it play over and over until we found ourselves humming it. That sweet song would prove to be instrumental in our lives even years down the road.

By the 2nd day, I was totally paralyzed and numb to well-above the waist. Doctors began blood transfusions of what they called "healthy antibodies" for 8 hours a day, 5 days a week, and pushed what appeared to be clear gelatin into my veins. Did I mention my veins did not like this process AT ALL? So, in rebellion, they exploded on a regular basis, covering my arms and hands with a beautiful rainbow of colors.

Oh, and let's don't forget my eyes. One of the wonderful side effects of G-B is blindness. Oh yeah, it's true. Because you can't blink, your corneas can dry out and you go blind. *So, it's not enough I have to have someone taking care of my most intimate hygiene needs? Now, I have to worry about going BLIND!?!*

During the waking hours, my mom would put drops in my eyes every 30 minutes. At night, the nurse would fill my eyes with a salve and tape them shut to avoid drying out – because I couldn't blink! Yeah, that was fun!! Had my first – of several – panic attacks. Waking up, not knowing where in the world I was and screaming my head off.

I should have known that first day I was in for a serious ride when that ER doc told me two very unusual things – *your children can come in to ICU whenever they want to see you and your mom can stay with you in the ICU room.* I thought *"what a nice hospital".* **Uh, no!** He knew that due to my rapid decline I could be tubed at any moment and having my mom with me would help me AND them!! That woman missed her calling! She's the best nurse you ever saw!!

As I waded through the humiliation of being hand-fed, toileted, bathed and looking like a 35-yr. old stroke patient lying there drooling, I had the added pleasure of the oxygen sensors. My fellow G-B survivors know, as the wave of numbness and paralysis spreads from your extremities into your torso, all of your autonomic nervous system begins to malfunction. *Auto what?* That's those vital functions like BREATHING and your HEART BEAT. Yes, I was hooked up to this machine that monitored my breathing through a wonderful beeping sound. One would think, *why don't you just turn off the beeping?* Well, then when the autonomic nervous system malfunctions and you STOP breathing, no one would know and you would D-I-E!! Now, you get it?!

Let's review. Drooling. Eyes wide open. Can't move. Can't feel. BEEEEEEPPPPP!!!!! My mom yells, *"BREATHE!!!!"* And then, with everything I can muster, I GASP for a breath!! Beeping stops. And then, we rewind and repeat. About every half hour, for *days*.

At the same time, the lung specialist is telling me that I will have to be tubed (placed on a ventilator) "tomorrow" if my oxygen level decreases by one point. Talk about motivation! If you still have an ounce of fight left, believe me THAT will bring it to the forefront. So, I drooled and gasped and lay there like a flopping fish. All the while, the beeping continued, the blood pressure cuff and the circulation boots squeezed and released, the immunoglobulin (clear gelatin) pushed into my blood stream and my veins continued to explode.

Then, there's what I called the "electric shock" treatment. With the purpose of stimulating your nerves to regenerate or wake up or whatever, they stick all these electrodes up and down your legs – thigh to ankle – and then shock the devil out of you! It's unbelievable – I'm not even sure it's legal in some countries! (Yes, it actually is – I checked!) It hurt so badly, I would lay there and tears would just roll down my face the whole time. Being one of those strange people that have an incredibly high pain tolerance, my mom knew if I was crying, it had to be horrific. And it was, every single day they did it. Yes, it was every day. And the visitors continued to stop by "just to see a Guillain-Barre patient".

As the resident "learning channel" patient for G-B, my room became a training ground for all staff hired within the last 25 years. Truthfully, I didn't mind. They had never seen G-B and had only book knowledge of its affects prior to my arrival. Each visitor would graciously request permission to come in before asking me questions about G-B. Truly the guinea pig really doesn't mind the inquisitive eyes – only the annoyance of the poking and prodding.

Are you afraid? I was asked that question quite often. My first response was "No, not really." But truthfully, I was terrified. Not of death. God had settled that question on Day 2. Lying in that bed, I had asked God, *"Am I gonna die?"* He clearly said, *"No, not now."* Then, my next question was *"Will I walk again?"*

He didn't speak to me to answer that one. Instead, He gave me a picture of myself. I was standing on a platform speaking to a group of people. It was like I was standing behind myself. So I couldn't see my face but I could see I was *standing.* That gave me something to hold onto when the doctors kept telling me I needed to "prepare for permanent disability". As I lay in that ICU bed, hooked up to all the beeping machines, I would hold that picture in my mind of myself STANDING on that platform. I'd like to say I was able to do that because I had *supreme faith.* That would be a lie. Honestly, I just wouldn't accept the alternative. *Couldn't accept it.* So what was I afraid of?

Lesson 5: Fear

What are <u>you</u> afraid of? If we are totally honest, we are **all** afraid of something. Besides the more common fears, we may be afraid of losing someone or something in our life.   This woman knew she was afraid but didn't even know yet of what! So, what do you do with that?!

In the 43rd chapter of Isaiah, the prophet shared a word from God containing a dual message. God said, *"When you pass through the waters, I will be with you, and when you pass through the rivers, they will not sweep over you. When you walk through the fire, you will not be burned; the flames will not set you ablaze."*

The first message is a confirmation that we WILL face different levels of battles – waters, rivers, fire, flames. The second message is that of a loving father imparting comfort to a child, reassuring us of not only His presence but His protection. When you *pass through* the rivers…when you *walk through* the fire…God tells us we WILL make it through. He goes on to say in verse 5, *"Do not be afraid, for I am with you…"*

We will face battles in this life that will cause us to fear. We WILL make it through if we remember we have a loving Father that will walk with us, and carry us through the fire.

Lesson 6

WHERE'S YOUR SMILE?

Day 2 was one of the hardest for all of us, but especially the children. When my children came for their first visit, Ethan, 5, ran over and jumped right up in the middle of my stomach. His loud, *"Mommy, what's WRONG with you?"* echoed down the hall. As I tried to explain in preschool terms how my body wasn't working right today, he was completely captivated with all the gadgets. Fearless in every aspect of his life, it never occurred to him that this was anything other than a temporary situation. On the other hand, Emily, 3 at the time, was seeing an entirely different picture. Upon first glance into my expressionless face, she buried her head in her daddy's shirt and refused to look at me at all.

When asked what was wrong, she tearfully stated, *"Mommy's mad at me."* Tears began to run down my face as I realized that my precious babies would be most affected by this horrible experience. My son's fearless faith in everything being conquerable would be tossed about and waver. My daughter's innocent hope in a smile and a hug making everything alright would be tested and probably torn. *What can I do or say God to give these babies their mommy back?*

In that instant, God gave me an idea. I said, *"Baby girl, mommy's not mad at you. My smile just isn't working today. Why don't we use our hands to smile until mommy's smile gets fixed?"* Then, using both hands – because my fingers were no longer working right either – I held my three middle fingers down on my right hand, extended my pinky and thumb, and pressed my hand up to my mouth. I looked at my beautiful babies and said, *"See? Mommy's still smiling!"* My daughter peeked out, grinned and began to make the same "hand smile" with her little hands. It became our way to smile at each other for the weeks to come.

Day 3 wasn't much better than Day 2. After the children left, I had plenty of time to think about my smile. I had asked God about dying. I had asked Him whether I would be the same again and saw myself STANDING. So that was good, right?

Not good enough. That's what the enemy said. *Not good enough. You didn't see your FACE! You don't know what you will look like!!*

Would I smile again?

Then, around lunch time, my dad walked into my ICU room. For most of my life, people have told me, *"You look just like your daddy!"* By that, they mean we share the same big grin that lights up our whole face and turns our eyes into rainbows. Dad was a full-time pastor at the time in a small South Georgia town. He was unable to make it to Atlanta until Day 3. When he walked into my room, the first thing he said was, *"How's my girl?"* Tears began to roll down my expressionless face as I replied, *"Daddy, I can't smile."* At that point, everyone in the room began to cry. He tried to encourage me like he always had. Looking to the bright side of every situation. But it was one of the hardest days in the whole process.

I had realized my greatest fear. Losing myself. Having walked a life of almost total control, I now had no control over anything. Not even my smile. Would I ever be the same again? *And Lord, will I smile again?*

I was acutely aware of my somber, sagging face. Each day as my mom helped me brush my teeth, I gazed into the mirror at a face I no longer recognized. Unable to blink or move any part of my face, I had the appearance of someone who really didn't care about anything. My face said, *"I'm neither happy to see you nor sad to see you go. I just really don't care!"*

I began to realize that my facial expression – or lack of – was being reciprocated by my attending nurse. She was a "grandma" in age and appearance. One would expect her to be loving and caring in nature. Quite the contrary! Her mannerisms were brisk and careless, her attitude rude and harsh. She would arrive on the scene each morning with not a word nor a smile. Just began her daily routine of tossing me left and right to change the sheets, stripping off my clothes with barely a grunt. By the time she was finished, I felt like I'd been mugged or worse. After a couple of days of this same behavior – and our ill-fated attempts at cordial conversation – my mom reached the end of her patience. As I watched my mom turn into a protective Mama Bear, stating *"She is NOT gonna treat my baby like this again"*, I believe God gave me an unexpected dose of mercy. (I say "unexpected" because I'm not merciful by nature.)

I said, *"Maybe something is wrong with her. I mean, maybe she thinks I'm mad at her because I'm not smiling!!"* My mom's dainty little *"Hmph!"* made me smile (in my head of course).

Barely a moment passed before God gave me a chance to try out my theory. The nurse came in, began tugging and pulling on me again without a word, and I said, *"I'm sorry I can't smile."* Her head jerked up and she said, *"What did you say?"* I replied, *"I said I'm sorry I can't smile. Normally I'm all smiles!! But I have this thing that has killed the nerves in my face so I can't even smile now. I just didn't want you to think I was mad at you or anything."*

That poor little lady stood there looking at me, dumbstruck for a full minute. Then, very slowly tears began to fill her eyes and roll down her cheeks. She said, *"Honey, I'm sorry. It's not you at all. You see, about three months ago, I lost my husband. We were married for over 40 years and then he died. When we got married, he had two adorable little children. They were just 2 and 3 years old and I raised them and loved them just like they were my own. When their daddy died a few months ago, I guess they blamed me or something. They took my house – the house we had lived in our whole marriage – and all our things."* She held up her little hand and said, *"They even took the wedding ring their daddy gave me, and my heart has just been broken."*

Well, needless to say, we were ALL crying by this time. Mom and I hugged her and told her how sorry we were. Even prayed with her right there in ICU. Prayed that

God would open those kids' eyes and heal her broken heart.

I saw living proof that day that God can use EVERY horrible thing the enemy throws our way and turn it around for good. He can even use my expressionless face to minister to a broken heart. That dear, sweet, grandma-nurse became one of the **best** nurses I had – and I had a lot of awesome nurses during my stay.

But Lord, will I <u>ever</u> smile again?

Lesson 6: Hoping Beyond Hope

What is hope? Paul tells us that *"hope that is seen is no hope at all."* (Romans 8:24) Webster's dictionary says hope is "a feeling that what is wanted will happen; desire accompanied by expectation." Simply put, if we can see it, we don't NEED hope.

This woman was facing some intimidating obstacles – paralysis, loss of function and way of life. Yet, she seemed to hope. She seemed to continue to believe that things would get better. She hoped beyond hope.

Paul continued in Romans 8:24-25 to tell us more about hope. He wrote, *"Who hopes for what he already has? If we hope for what we do not yet have, we wait for it patiently."*

Ahhh. Now that's hoping beyond hope. *Lord, help me to never give up hope!*

Lesson 7

HOME AT LAST

Finally on Day 8, just when I thought I couldn't take it anymore, the numbness began to subside. The paralysis began to be replaced by a thick "sleep" feeling. The feeling began to come back into my face and upper body, and I could actually SMILE. Well, it was just a hint of a smile. Kind of a smirk really but I was working it. I could now sit up and feed myself without making too big of a mess. Then, on the afternoon of Day 9, I was released to go home. HOME.

I couldn't believe I was home! I was still numb above the knee and my face looked like I'd had a stroke, but I was home! The daily bed therapy that I had received in the hospital seemed to have worked. Although I stumbled a bit, I could walk short distances again. I knew I was on the road to a full recovery. And I was home.

For the first time in a while, it was just us. Friends had brought supper and my mom got us all settled before she finally headed home to her house after her nine day "vacation" in ICU. My husband bathed me, dressed me, got me into bed and then got the kids in bed. For the first time in over a week, I slept in my own bed.

Home.

Lesson 7: What is Home?

Have you ever moved? Been evicted? Lost your home?
Always heard that trite little expression "home is where
the heart is." *What does that even mean?*

Sometime between diagnosis and day 8, I believe this
woman probably figured that out. In chapter 3 in the
book of Colossians, Paul and Timothy had figured it out.
They encouraged the folks *"set your hearts on things
above...set your minds on things above, not on earthly
things."*

Jesus told us in the book of Matthew, chapter 6, verses
19-21, *"do not store up for yourselves treasures on
earth...but store up for yourselves treasures in heaven."*
He reminded us *"where your treasure is, there your heart
will be also."*

We spend so much time and energy saving up, building
up, stocking up – *for what?* In a matter of moments, all
those things can be gone, wiped away. And then what?

Then, we get a close look at what *really* matters – like this
woman did. Jesus told us clearly not to worry about what
we would eat or drink or what we would wear. In other
words, those earthly things should not be our priority. He
told us to seek Him and His ways and all those other
things would be added as we needed them.   (Matthew
6:25-33)

*What do **you** treasure? If you woke up one day and all the
earthly treasures you have accumulated were gone, what
would still be there? WHO would still be there?*

Tami L. Sanders

At the End of My Rope

Tami L. Sanders

Lesson 8

IT'S BACK!!

We had been told to "expect a relapse" but rebuked that in the name of Jesus and believed we were "covered". So when I woke up that next morning to find the numbness had returned, I stumbled to the bathroom totally terrified of what I was going to see. Staring back at me in the mirror was that stony, expressionless monster of a face. No smile.

As my husband held me in his arms, I just sobbed, *"I don't think I can do this again."* With tears running down his cheeks, he bravely replied, *"Yes, we can."* And then we prayed, called my parents, packed up the children and headed back to the ICU.

I think the second round was actually worse than the first because I knew what to expect. I knew how many veins were going to blow in the process of receiving the healthy antibodies. I knew how much the electrodes were going to hurt during the "electric shock" therapy. I had already experienced the humiliation of being fed, bathed and toileted. Yet, here I was again, totally helpless.

As I looked into the faces of the nurses and staff, I actually believe they were as sad to see me back as I was to be there. They had celebrated my victory of going home. And now I was back, and seemingly, just as bad off as I was before.

So, together we started Round Two – of everything. The IVs, breathing treatments, physical therapy, constant monitoring. Mom even got her bed back – she was "thrilled" of course. And we brought the music – that was the only redeeming factor. 24/7 worship songs playing in the ICU. Actually, another redeeming factor was all my wonderful nurses and attendants were back. We had grown to know each other better than some families. And they treated me like family. Lots of love and encouragement was poured on me – helping to cover the sting of the needles and humiliation of intimate care.

Lesson 8: Losing Heart

You've faced and beaten a cancer diagnosis only to be told *"It's back."* You weathered that last storm of adultery, had forgiven and moved forward – *now again?!* The list could go on and on.

It's so easy to lose heart in the face of another battle, especially when you were so certain you'd finally beaten that enemy once and for all. *So what do you do?*

We must go back to the beginning. The basics of our faith. The same God that raised Jesus from the dead will also raise us to new life. In 2nd Corinthians, chapter 4, verses 16-18, Paul encouraged the Corinthians not to lose heart. He said, *"Though outwardly we are wasting away, yet inwardly we are being renewed day by day. Our light and momentary troubles (when compared with what Christ suffered) are achieving for us an eternal glory that far outweighs them all. So we fix our eyes NOT on what is seen, but on what is unseen. For what is seen is temporary, but what is unseen is eternal."*

I guess the simplest way to not lose heart is to keep the main thing the main thing! Set our eyes and our hope on Jesus. When the battle rages around us, threatening to consume us, we set our eyes on Jesus and hold fast to His hand. Hold tight to the promises He has given to us. He is *always* faithful.

Lesson 9

Deja Vu

Have you ever seen the movie "Groundhog Day"? In that movie, the lead actor keeps waking up to repeat the day, again and again. We used to call that a déjà vu – been here, done that. That's how the next 10 days went for me. A continual feeling of "been here, done that" was all over everything. The unfair part was that I had NO desire to repeat it! Wasn't like I could "fix" it by repeating it!!

There's really no antidote for G-B. So the only thing the medical team can do is to infuse your blood stream with healthy antibodies and keep your vital organs going while your body fights to regain control of the neurological system. The numbness and lack of mobility were again head to toe. Yet we still began this second round with a second spinal tap, just to "be sure" it was indeed G-B. *Really?* More "goop" in my eyes, oxygen mask, IVs, blood pressure cuffs, circulation boots – only to be removed when the electrodes were placed for the "shock" therapy.

Not a pretty picture. *Is anything in ICU?* Visitors were limited to family and the closest of friends. And pastors, of course. That was ok with me. Nobody really understood anyway. I mean, if you haven't been in that spot, how could you understand? I barely understood it all myself. How does one lose all their dignity and self-respect in just one day?

Doctors and nurses would peer over me and say, *"That's similar to a stroke." "A bit like Lou Gehrig's." "I think it's more like…"* Our brains try so hard to fill in the blanks of those things that make no sense to us. I've done it a million times. Yet, when it's all said and done, we still really understand only a small part of what makes up the human body. I found out though that some people DO understand. Up close and personal. Through their own personal tragedy.

Lesson 9: Rewind

Back in the days of cassette tapes, I used to love to listen to my favorite part of a song over and over again. I would listen to it, singing at the top of my lungs, then just press "rewind" and do it all over again.

As much as I loved repeating that chorus over and over, there are some things that I really wouldn't want to repeat. Mistakes. Bad days. Bad relationships. And those things that fall into the category of "personal tragedy". Many of you have had situations in your own life that feel like a déjà vu – they just keep painfully repeating. *So what do you do?*

In 1st Samuel, Hannah prayed, *"It is not by strength that we prevail…"* I believe what she was saying is that it's not by MY strength that I will prevail. The woman with Guillain-Barre told us in Lesson 2 she had always stood on the scripture, *"I can do all things through Christ who strengthens me"*, believing at that time that Christ was refilling her tank to go on. I believe the scripture more accurately presents a picture of Christ's strength to do all things through us when we are totally dependent on Him. We must *"forget what is behind and strain to see what is ahead"* – we must leave the past *(even the recent past)* in the past and focus our attention on what God wants for us **today**. Paul told the folks at Philippi to *"press on toward the goal"* if they wanted to win the prize that God had for them. (Philippians 3:12-15)

I don't think it was politeness that caused Paul to tell those people that he had not perfected in his own life what he was instructing them to do. He knew, and he wanted them to know, that this process of setting the past aside to stay focused on the present was not an easy thing. And it would *not* be a one-time process.

If we want to move forward, and make it through the many trials and struggles of life, we must learn to press "rewind". We don't rewind the past problems and mistakes. Instead we rewind and repeat the process of letting go and moving forward in faith and hope, secure in God's ability to carry us through.

Lesson 10

I GET IT

Truly I don't remember whether she came during Round One or Round Two. I only remember the look on her face and how it changed my life.

Before G-B entered my life, I'd been active in our children's ministry at church. Working side by side with a husband-wife pastoral team, I had the pleasure to serve with two married couples in an extremely rewarding ministry to kids. The wives and I got really close and chatted about most everything. Both a bit younger than me, I felt almost a sister bff bond with them both. The older of the two was a lot like me, silly, fun, outgoing – we got along like two peas in a pod. The younger was a bit more serious, about everything. To be fair, she'd had some serious "stuff" happen in her life. So, the Christian thing to do would have been to show grace and mercy. Oh, but not me! Remember up to this point, I'd led a charmed life – nothing beyond my control. My face said "grace" but my heart said *"Get over it!"* No grace or mercy there. Until that day when she came into my ICU room.

When you're feeling and looking your worst, there is one person above all you really don't want to see. That is the person you've judged harshly. And in she walked, right up to the side of my bed. She came in with the lady children's pastor. While the children's pastor engaged my mom in conversation, she came to my bedside and said *"How ya doing?"* I bravely said, *"I'm fine."*

My God, what a ridiculous thing to say! I'm lying here hooked up to everything, looking like a 35 year-old stroke patient and I'm FINE?!

Then she looked me straight in the eyes and said, *"No, I mean tell me what's going on!"* Knowing she wasn't going to let me get by without the truth – one thing I really admired about her – I began to recount the details. The spinal taps, the blood transfusions, the electric shock, the panic attacks. Then, the humiliation – the bathing, toileting, feeding. When I got to what I thought was the end of the list, I glanced back to her face. That's when I saw it – *painful recognition.* Her childhood years, of battling leukemia and all that went with it, were still a present and painful memory almost 15 years later. She understood, up close and personal. And now, I did too.

In that moment, God changed my heart. I realized in that split second that each one of us play on the same field. And at some point in each of our lives, we will feel like we are barely hanging on. We will ask the question, *"Am I gonna make it through this?"* And in that moment, we will do one of two things. We will either draw closer to God or we will turn away from Him totally.

I Choose You, Lord.

That day changed my life. About a year later, I called

my friend and apologized for my arrogance and lack of mercy toward her private pain. Thankfully, God shielded her because she said she'd never felt it. *Thank you Lord.* She graciously granted me permission to share the story. A year later I would write a short story about it entitled *"Through His Eyes".* God used my friend and her personal triumph to change my heart. *Thank you dear friend. Thank you Lord.*

I began to look at people differently after that. It seemed to open my eyes to what people actually must be going through to do the things they do. Little did I know then that even years later when I would want to look at someone and judge them harshly, God would remind me of that day. He would remind me to look at them through His eyes. *God had changed my heart.*

Lesson 10: A New Heart

When someone has a heart transplant, it takes a certain amount of time for the doctors to know whether the body of the recipient is actually going to accept the new heart. There are times when the new healthy heart is rejected and the sick person either has to get a second heart or death follows.

With our spiritual heart, it's a bit different. We are born with a sick heart, full of selfishness and pride – sinful. We look at others and judge them harshly in an attempt to make ourselves look and feel better. We figure if we are "doing better than him" then we must be ok.

God looks at things a bit differently. He says, *"Do not*

judge. You too will be judged." In Matthew, He goes a step further and tells us that we *"will all give an account on the day of judgment."* In the book of Hebrews, Paul told us that God *"judges the thoughts and the attitudes."*

Well, then we are ALL out of luck, right? **Exactly.**

This woman realized at this point the error of her ways. She had lived a life filled with pride and had been unable to see the people around her with love or compassion. She needed a new heart – a spiritual heart.

The prophet Ezekiel shared a word from God with the people of Israel. He told them- chapter 36, verses 25-26 – God said, *"I will sprinkle clean water on you and you will be clean; I will cleanse you from all your impurities and from all your idols. I will give you a new heart and put a new spirit in you; I will remove from you your heart of stone and give you a heart of flesh."*

God further explains what will happen when the people receive a new heart. He tells them they will have a desire to follow Him, to obey Him. This is not a fleshly heart that the body will reject. When God gives us a new spiritual heart, we are *moved* to leave the past behind – or changed from the inside out. 2nd Corinthians 5:17 states, *"If anyone is in Christ, he is a new creation; the old has gone, the new has come!"*

Lord, change my heart.

Lesson 11

HOME AGAIN

After three weeks in the hospital, I was able to come home. This trip home included some lifestyle changes. I could no longer walk on my own. No longer stand without assistance. The doctor had used some words we never want to hear. *Permanently disabled.*

My mom and my best friend had twenty-four hour care lined up before I walked in the front door of my home. Truly, they had a schedule written out for shifts covering the first two weeks. Friends of mine from church were with me from the time my husband left for work. They were all amazing!! They cooked our meals, cleaned the house, did our laundry, played with kids and made certain that I didn't "forget and try to get up". When my husband got home in the evening, the kids were bathed and they had supper cooked. Once they ensured we were settled and eating supper, they just slipped out. Then, they were back again the next day.

It was a crazy time.

The children were thrilled to have mommy home. They would not leave my side. My daughter and I no longer had to use our hands to smile. I couldn't stand but I could smile. ☺ So she bounced around all over the house like the sun was shining once again. My son somehow had grown into a mighty warrior during my hospital stay. He positioned himself at my side or at my feet almost every waking moment. It was as if he was standing guard so that "enemy" wouldn't sneak up on us again.

After two weeks, we released our friends to go back to their normal lives while we tried to create our new life, post G-B.

Lesson 11: Struck Down but Not Destroyed

Home had a different feel this time. Having been here before, only to leave again, she was a bit more focused on creating a new life than walking in any sense of overt optimism. We can sense the hope is still there but may be wearing a bit thin.

Believe it or not, we are supposed to walk prepared for this too. God told us we were to *"let Light shine out of darkness"* – which means **expect** some darkness.

In 2nd Corinthians 4:7-9, Paul calls us jars of clay. He tells us that when we shine the Light of the glory of God even in the midst of the darkest moments, it's only then that we can show the power is coming from God and not us. Paul triumphantly declares, *"We are hard pressed on every side but not crushed; perplexed but not in despair; persecuted but not abandoned; struck down but not destroyed."*

Life presses in. God ensures we are not crushed. We may be perplexed (not understand) what is going on but we don't have to despair. People and situations may cause us to feel persecuted. God will never abandon us. We may be struck down. With God, we will not be destroyed.

Lesson 12

A NEW ROUTINE

We had a lot of things to get used to with this "new" mommy. This mommy couldn't stand up without assistance. She definitely couldn't walk. It was so important to me to create a safe place for the kids. I made certain I never showed weakness in front of them, emotionally at least. No tears. No complaining. So everything became a game.

Like the day I forgot about my new impairment and bent over to pick up a string off the carpet and fell out of the chair. We played a two-hour game of "push the cushions under mommy" until I was high enough to drag myself onto the couch. When we did laundry, Ethan would climb up onto my lap in the wheelchair, pull himself up onto the washer and hang into the machine to drag out the wet clothes. Then, all smiles he would throw them down to Emily – sometimes AT Emily. She would collapse into giggles as she tossed them into the dryer. I would clap and squeal in a thrilled mommy-voice, letting them know they were doing a great job. *So what if a couple of things hit the floor?*

When we needed food or drink, Ethan would again climb up into my lap, pull himself up onto the counter and walk the countertop until he found the right cabinet. Yes, I actually taught my son to climb on the counters. *So what if we had footprints on the countertop?* I would later have to help him "unlearn" that talent. ☺

In years to come, other moms would ask me how I trained my kids to clean their rooms and pick up after themselves. With a smile, I would tell them we started really young. Sometimes I would fill in the sad details that involved two little children losing their childhood innocence because of a thing called Guillain-Barre. But more often than not, I'd just let them know how very blessed I was to have such amazing children.

One of the new things we had to learn was some healthy boundaries. Not being able to walk while parenting two preschoolers brings a whole new challenge. We were blessed to have a fenced in back yard with a playset for the kids to enjoy. Safety! A few moments of bliss for a mother. Until the day I rolled up to the back door, looked out the sliding glass door and only saw one child.

Ethan had always been my speedy child. From the time he learned to walk, if you blinked, he was gone. If you missed him, just grab a wet washcloth. He was either feeding his baby sister Oreos on the kitchen floor or dousing her head with baby powder, on top of the petroleum jelly he had covered her with! Every day was always an exciting event!

My first test for a new sitter was *"If they go in opposite directions, which one do you grab first?"* The sitter usually said, *"Emily!"* because she was the little one. *Oh no! Go for Ethan!!* I knew Ethan would be a block down the street while Emily, sweet little "stop and smell the roses" child that she was, would probably be right where you left her.

That afternoon, when I looked out and only saw Emily, I quickly slid open the door, and said, *"Emily, where's Ethan?"* She calmly pointed to my right and said, *"Over there."* I leaned forward in my wheelchair. No Ethan. I said, *"Emily, where is Ethan??"* She looked up again – like I was interrupting her playtime – and said, *"Mommy, he's over there!"* Again, she pointed to my right. I leaned and looked. No Ethan. Very carefully, I used every bit of strength I had and dragged myself to my feet, holding onto the doorframe tightly. I looked around the yard. No Ethan. I hollered now, *"EMILY, Where's Ethan?!"* She jumped to her feet, pointed and said, *"Mommy, he's in the tree!"* As I looked up, there he was about 25 feet up a pine tree. My precious 5-year old - who I had taught to climb - had climbed the chain linked fence, shinnied up the pine tree and was sitting triumphantly on a limb smaller than my forearm.

That's one of those mommy moments when you want to scream at the top of your lungs but know if you do a catastrophe will follow. So, I very calmly – faking it of course – said, *"Ethan Sanders, you carefully come down right this minute."* His *"ok"* could barely be heard as he slid down the trunk of the tree and dropped about 12 feet to the ground like he was a Marine jumping out of a plane. Oh, he was proud! And I was thankful. *Thank you Lord.* Then we made a new boundary of not climbing trees without mommy's permission.

Lesson 12: Making Lemonade

Ever just get tired of fighting? I don't mean fighting with people but fighting situations, battles. Do you ever just get tired of having to face some sort of battle EVERY single day? *Why do I get so many lemons and have to make lemonade?*

I hear people say "It's always *something*, right?" Unfortunately, there is always some new battle to fight. If it's not money, it's health issues. If you're feeling good and have your bills all paid, you're probably having trouble at work. Or maybe at home. *I'm so tired.*

As a believer, is it ok to say that?

It must be. Jesus said in Matthew 11:28-30, *"Come to me, all you who are weary and burdened, and I will give you rest.* (Lord, that's me!) *Take my yoke upon you and learn from me, for I am gentle and humble in heart, and you will find rest for your souls. For my yoke is easy and my burden is light."*

Learn WHAT from Jesus? Maybe we can learn that because Jesus humbled himself and admitted He needed His father, God, He was able to make it through the most horrific situations and trials. Maybe we could learn to be an ox! *Huh?*

Jesus twice referred to a "yoke" and said His yoke was easy – His burden was light. Now, I know a bit about farming and a yoke is a seriously big piece of wood that sits across the neck of an ox. It is NOT a small or "light" thing at all. But the cool thing about a yoke is that it's made for TWO oxen, not one ox.   When Jesus made the reference to the yoke being easy and light, I believe He was reminding us that HE would be with us. Jesus carries the weight of the yoke for us, making it lighter for us to bear.

Pretty cool, right?

There's only one hitch!

We have to make sure we are "yoked" with Jesus. The only way for Jesus to lighten our load and bear our burdens is for us to join our wagon to His. Just like two people are "yoked" or "hitched" in a marriage relationship, we must be "yoked" to Christ in a personal relationship. Then, and only then, will we receive the rest for our soul that Jesus spoke about.

Thank you, Jesus, for bearing my burdens.

Lesson 13

NOT ALL FUN AND GAMES

The months that followed were definitely not all fun and games. My physical therapist came three days a week and did bed therapy. She basically got me up and dressed on those days then helped me exercise my legs and arms for the next couple of hours. Our first goal was to get me strong enough to be able to stand unassisted for 5 seconds. Yes, that is not a misprint. Five Seconds.

She was so patient. A Christian herself. We talked a lot about faith while we exercised. I say "we" exercised because she got as good of a workout as I did. It's no wonder PTs stay in such great shape. We worked and worked. Still I couldn't do it. I think I made it 2 or 3 seconds one day. *Gotta get to 5 seconds!*

The doctor had released me from care – *MMI* he said. Maximum Medical Improvement. Basically, this is a politically correct way to say "we've done all we can do and you're as good as we expect you to get". I didn't receive this prognosis spiritually, of course. I was still hanging on to the picture God had given me of myself standing, speaking. However, the harsh reality was I had to deal with the earthly realities of everyday life.

Our first vacation was a valiant attempt at normalcy. We decided we needed to get out of town – get away from everything. *Let's go to the mountains!* So, we headed to Gatlinburg Tennessee for a weekend getaway. A thousand times we would say to each other, *"Whose idea was this?"* but we did have some fun. Challenging but fun.

It was fun – or should I say funny – when they turned loose of my wheelchair long enough to open a shop door and I began to roll backwards down the hill. I screamed, they screamed, everyone screamed. It was fun getting a woman who couldn't stand in and out of a moving chair lift. Seriously though, it was truly fun to see the kids interacting in a normal environment with other people for the first time in months.

The stares brought me back to another reality of my new normal. As I gazed into the face in the mirror, *the right side of her face hung mostly limp like she'd had a stroke. Her mouth drooped on one side, giving the appearance of someone much older. Her hair was dull and lifeless, as if no one had known how to make it better. As I watched her in that chair, the woman's frail appearance made it clear she HAD to be there. Her eyes held a deep sadness and more than a bit of worry. Her hands and fingers, drawn and weak, were of no help in pushing herself. The little girl stayed by her mother's side, helping with every need, trying to block the opening to the door in an attempt to maintain her mother's dignity. Everyone noticed the woman could barely transfer herself from the chair to the toilet. Who is she? And what happened to her? I couldn't help but wonder what had turned such a young woman with a beautiful family into this lifeless portrait of an old lady. As I looked at her in the mirror, she looked back – straight into my eyes. I immediately turned away. It was almost painful to look at her. But I seemed to be drawn back to her eyes – those haunted, sad eyes, filled with the memories of the monster that had stolen her youth and that of her children. As I stared into those pain-filled eyes, I thought to myself,* **"I'm the lady in the wheelchair."**

I learned a lot in that chair. I learned that not everything that says "Handicap Accessible" truly is! Bathrooms are small. Doorways are smaller. Some folks don't know what to say. So they just don't speak to you at all. Some folks don't even look at you! I had servers ask my husband, *"What does SHE want?"* I would surprise them and say, *"SHE wants....."* and watch them gasp. Now that was funny!

Then, there's the folks that speak especially loud, like you're hard of hearing, or the ones that speak especially S-L-O-W. The kids would look at me with that expression that said, *"Are they ok?"* It was quite surreal at times but we all pressed on.

Lesson 13: Wake Up!

Ever had one of those moments when you wish someone would just slap you and say, "WAKE UP!" Then, you suddenly realize that you ARE awake and this STUFF, this horrible, unbelievable situation is **REAL**.

Lord, what do I do with that?

We cannot begin to comprehend what Jesus must have felt in the garden, faced with His impending crucifixion, when He asked His Father *"take this from me"*. Yet, how often have I asked God to take something from me? To pluck me out of a situation that seemed beyond my ability to bear.

Then, I remember…He KNOWS how I feel. He truly understands my broken heart. My tormented spirit. My weary state of mind. Yet, in the middle of His most horrible night, He submitted His will to His Father's.

How do I do that?

The only way we can do that is to follow Jesus example. *So what did He do?* Jesus finished praying *"not My will but Yours"* and both Matthew and Mark wrote, *"Then, He returned to the disciples…"* In Luke's gospel he wrote, *"…He rose from prayer…"*

What did Jesus do? He left the STUFF there and got up!

What should we do when faced with an unsurmountable obstacle? A moment so horrible we just pray to WAKE UP. We need to talk to God about it, lay it before Him and trust Him to work it out, and then **we get up**. We *leave it with Him*, and we emotionally, mentally, spiritually, and physically (if possible), ***GET UP!***

Easy? No.

Simple? **Yes!**

Pray. Lay it down. Get up and leave it there.

Lesson 14

LET'S ALL STAND...

I don't think I ever realized how many things involve standing. Things I took for granted. Showering for example. Yes, we got one of those wonderful shower chairs but let's be honest. It is not the same! There's something about standing and letting the hot water run down your head, down your back, right down to your feet. It's just not the same in a chair.

And dancing. I didn't realize how many times during the course of a day that I do this little dance. Maybe a song comes into my head or on a commercial. Just makes me start to dance a little dance. Umm, standing!

Praise and Worship was really hard. I should say it was a learning experience. I learned how very much I had taken for granted STANDING to praise the Lord. As the music would start and people would rise to their feet, I would begin to cry. Not messy loud crying – it's church after all. Just the slow, quiet tears that you want to hide but tells everyone your heart is broken. And my heart was broken that I could no longer stand and sing. *Keep the faith girl!*

I hear you Lord. Yes, I must keep believing. I have a lot to be thankful for – I can SMILE again!! And I **will** stand again. I will **walk** again. One day.

Lesson 14: Name Them One by One

Growing up, my parents instilled a deep love for hymns in my soul. Those old, dear songs whose lyrics came straight from the scriptures. As a child, most of the scripture I knew was in the form of a song. One of my folks' favorite songs has the verse *"Count Your Many Blessings, Name Them One by One. Count Your Many Blessings, See What God Has Done."* At the time I learned that song, it really meant very little to me. Just a song with catchy words, written to a memorable tune.

I have since realized the true meaning and worth of those words. *Name them one by one. One by one.* We all have at least two things we can be thankful for, two blessings. On the day in memory, I had more than two blessings. I was alive. I could SMILE again. And I had the hope and vision of walking again.

Even in the darkest of hours, if we stop and listen, God will whisper and remind us of some of the many things we can count as blessings. *Well, what if I can't walk?* Can't smile. Have no family. Have no job. No home. *What if I can't think of a single thing to count as a blessing in my life?*

Bring it to Him. And then listen. You will quietly hear Him whisper, *"You have Me."* God loves each of us so much that He allowed His own Son to be broken and die on a cruel cross to provide a way for us to be made whole. (John 3:16) He loves you and me.

"Count your many blessings, name them one by one…"

A New Direction

Lesson 15

Where's Your Faith?

Isn't it just like the enemy to come to you when you're already down and ask you a question like that? You feel like you've been to hell and back, and are hanging on as tightly as you can to your faith. Then, right when you've just hit another wall, he comes to you and says, "Where's your faith?"

That's the way I felt that last Sunday – and every day leading up to it. I had been in faith-filled churches for most of my life. The kind of churches that truly believe God wants to heal and still has the power to heal. Those churches that teach the book of Acts like it's your daily manual to living a Christian life. Everyone I knew was praying and believing for my healing. Thousands of hands had been laid on me in faith. Believing for my miracle. The people around me were guarding their words as much as I was – only words of life and healing were being spoken over me.

Yet, that Sunday morning I sat in that chair, still unable to stand. *I believe Lord.* I will NOT believe otherwise. I'd like to tell you I had some great faith but that wouldn't be true. God truly was the only hope I had. I HAD to depend on Him. Now more than ever.

So again, I sat and sang. Cried a little. Smiled a lot.

And waited for my healing. That Sunday was a bit different. The pastor was sharing a couple was coming to **teach** about healing. *I don't need to LEARN about healing. I just need to be healed.* They were supposed to be well-known, though I'd never heard of them. We made plans to come.

Lesson 15: Don't Get Your Hopes Up

I hear you! There it was again. That voice in my head. *"Don't get your hopes up!"* You know what I mean. You see a glimmer of light at the end of that dark tunnel, only to be reminded of the dark days of the past.

So what do I do?

Well, let's see what the Book says. *"Ask and it will be given to you….Everyone who asks receives."* Matthew 7:8 *"Your faith has made you well."* Luke 17:19 *"If you have faith as small as a mustard seed…nothing shall be impossible to you."* Matthew 17:20

A mustard seed? Do you know how small a mustard seed really is? It's about the size of the head of a pencil. Now, let's get serious! That is NOT a whole lot of faith. *So, why do I waste so much time listening to the enemy's voice telling me not to get my hopes up?!*

Instead, today I will ask God to increase my faith to the size of that tiny little mustard seed and set my hopes on the impossible!?! Watch God turn the IM-possible into the POSSIBLE!!

Lesson 16

No Longer Just a Dream

Labor Day weekend, 1999. I'd been sitting in this chair for months, seemed like years. *Is tonight the night Lord?* I don't remember every detail of that night. The evangelists were a married couple in their early 80's who had been traveling the world for over 30 years teaching about healing. They didn't do anything strange. Just sat in a chair on the platform and taught what the Bible said about healing. For two hours, they read scriptures and talked about each one. They made it clear that healing was not about them or who may lay hands on you. It was all about God. His power. His decision who, when and how He healed.

At first, that kind of threw me. I thought, *Why would He want to heal ME?* I mean, my friend had been such a woman of God and battled breast cancer for 8 years and DIED. So why would God heal me and not her?

Did I say that out loud? It was almost like they heard me!

The man said, *"I can't tell you why your friend or relative did not receive healing on this earth or why they died. I can only tell you what the Word says. And the Bible clearly says God heals and He wants to heal you. So we're going to believe God, then let's see what He's going to do tonight."*

Then, he said, *"If you need healing, we want you to come forward. I am not going to pray for you or over you because I don't want any of you to think this is about me. This is about God and His power. So, you come forward and stand in front of any of these folks from your church. They are going to pray and we're going to see what God does."*

Since we'd dropped off the kids in the children's ministry, it was just my husband and me. He rolled me to the front and transferred me to the front pew right in front of the pastor and wife of the church. We had moved with my husband's job about a month after I got home from the hospital. So, we had been visiting this church now for about two months but were not members. Growing up in the church, I put a lot of faith in the pastor's role and calling. So, even though I didn't know this pastor well, I quickly made the decision that if the evangelist wasn't going to pray for me, I wanted the pastor to – yes, I ignored the part about it not mattering who prayed for you. Thank God, He met my faith where it was at!

The pastor's wife was a registered nurse and asked me about my diagnosis and what the doctor's prognosis had been. They listened attentively while I shared about the G-B and the prognosis of permanent nerve damage and long-term disability. And then, they began to pray. They prayed over each leg, each muscle group, the nerves, everything. They prayed for muscle mass to be restored and nerves to be healed and nerve function recreated. For about fifteen minutes, they prayed. And I sat.

Did I feel warmth? Heat? Tingling? Nope. None of that. I truly didn't feel a thing physically. I just had an overwhelming urge to GET UP!! When they asked me, *"Would you like to see if you can walk?"* I said, *"Yes I would."* They told me they would be right there if I needed them. They helped me stand to my feet, then slowly released my hands. Everyone stood with arms outstretched as if to catch me as I began to move.

Looking back, they say I walked like someone with two prosthetic limbs. I swung from the hips and moved each leg, still numb, staggering like a drunk person. I was walking!! People began to cheer and holler, *"Praise God!"* *"Hallelujah!!"* Everyone was clapping as I staggered back and forth across the front of the church. I continued to walk for about ten minutes before they made me sit me back down to rest. As I sat there smiling from ear to ear, all I could think was that it was no longer a dream. I could walk!!

Lesson 16: Celebrate the Mountaintops

How often have I gotten so concerned about what was to come that I missed the moment? Missed the opportunity to celebrate my mountaintop because I was concerned about what valley might lay ahead.

We are often reminded to be thankful in all things, all situations (1st Thessalonians 5:18). We are even reminded to be content, no matter our circumstance. (Philippians 4:11) Why are we so hesitant to spend time celebrating the mountaintops? I heard one young believer say recently, "I don't want to jinx it!" I quickly shared some biblical truth about the impossibility of jinxing anything when following the Lord.

God knew we would walk through valleys. Even climb some rocky slopes getting up to that mountaintop. He wants us to celebrate when we get there. Remember, He's walked with us every step of the way. Often carried us over the hardest parts of the journey. Celebrating the victory is a good thing. In fact, it's a GOD-thing.

James 1:17, *"Every good and perfect gift is from above."* David knew this. Abraham knew it. Moses knew it. The Israelites knew it. And they celebrated the moments of victory that God gave them. They celebrated the mountaintops.

Don't be afraid to celebrate the victorious moments that God gives you. Stand on that mountaintop and shout for joy, ***"Hallelujah!!"***

Shout for joy to the Lord, all the earth. Worship the Lord with gladness; come before Him with joyful songs. Know that the Lord is God. It is He who has made us, and we are His; we are His people, the sheep of His pasture. Enter His gates with thanksgiving and His courts with praise; give thanks to Him and praise His name. For the Lord is good and His love endures forever; His faithfulness continues through all generations. Psalms 100

Lesson 17

Mommy, What Did You Do?

There's nothing quite like seeing the joy of a miracle through the eyes of a child. I asked my husband to go get the children while I leaned against the wall in the front foyer of the church. I suddenly had no desire to ever sit again. When they came bounding into the foyer and saw me leaning against the wall, Ethan and Emily came running to me and said, *"Mommy what are you doing?"* I pointed toward the front windows and said, *"Go over there and look."* They ran to the windows, looking out and said, *"What are we looking for Mommy?"* I said, *"Look here at Mommy!"* As they turned back toward me, I began to walk, still swinging hip to hip, across the floor to them. They both began to jump up and down, shouting, *"Mommy! You're walking!! What did you do?"* With tears running down my face, I said, *"Mommy, didn't do it. God healed me!"* Their joy was not only heard and seen, it was mirrored. Everyone around began to cry and clap again. God had healed me. *Thank you Lord.*

The next day, therapy day, Ethan and Emily had an opportunity to see the same joy on the face of my therapist. We surprised her that day! The kids and I had it all planned out. I would stay in bed, just like normal, and wait for her to come help me get up. The children entertained her for a few minutes after she arrived to give me time to get in position. When they

could hold her no longer, I hollered, *"Ok, I'm ready."*
As she stood from the couch and started toward the
hallway, I came out the bedroom door and began to
walk down the hall toward her. She stopped, gasped
and began to shout. It was the adult version of Ethan
and Emily's joy the night before!

Over the next few weeks, we got the same response
from everyone who had known the story. I took the
opportunity to go back to the hospital to see those
precious people who had taken such incredible care of
me. I will never forget the reactions when I walked in
with a plate of brownies. I guess it's not everyday
someone walks back into ICU for a repeat visit. A
simple thank you will never be enough!

Then, there was the day I went back to see my
neurologist. One of the smartest doctors I've ever had
the privilege to know, he was missing only one thing –
Jesus. During my hospital stay, every time he would tell
me to prepare myself for my disability, I would smile
and say, *"I'm believing I will be healed."* He would smile
back, that professional smile that says, *"You have no clue!"*
Since he had released me on MMI (Maximum Medical
Improvement), I really had no medical reason to return.
But I made the appointment anyway. The look on his
face was priceless!! As I walked around the room, he
kept looking at me and then back at my chart. He
would flip through that 3" file, reading and scrutinizing
every detail. He'd say, *"How did this happen?"* I would
respond, *"God healed me, Doc."* He'd look at me again,
read some more, look back at me and shake his head.
He'd say again, *"I've never seen anything like this! How did
this happen?"* *"GOD HEALED ME DOC!"* That day

my doc was the one who got a clue of my God's awesome power!

Some things came back quickly, like my ability to drive. I found out you really **can** drive a car with a bit of neuropathy in your feet. Not recommended but do-able. Then, other things came back a bit more slowly, like coordination. For quite some time after my initial healing, I still walked like I had two prosthetic legs, swinging from the hip, side to side. One of my friends used to tease me and say, *"Walk this way!"* and he would walk alongside me, swinging side to side. He'd have me laughing so hard I would almost stumble. It took a while to be able to climb steps or gracefully manage a curb. Almost like I had to retrain myself to walk again.

Before long though, I was back to my old self, at least on the outside. I could walk without stumbling. I could bend and squat, without taking two hours to get up off the floor. I still had what is called *residual numbness* in the soles of my feet but I considered it a small blessing. I had asked God when I was healed to never let me forget what He had done, what He had brought me through. So each day when I put my feet on the floor and felt that tiny little bit of thickness on the bottoms of my feet, I was reminded of God's grace, His power and His love for me. I decided I'm ok with that.

So what about the inside? Was I back to my old self on the inside?

Lesson 17: The Gift or the Giver

How many times have you heard about someone making it through some life-threatening situation, only to hear it described as "lucky"? Or heard some other ridiculous source given the credit for something they had no part in?

Wow! That tornado just missed our house!! We were LUCKY!

They could have been killed!! Good thing he was such a good driver. They were so LUCKY!!

The tropical storm could have turned into a major hurricane. Mother Nature was smiling on us!

Cross your fingers!! Knock on wood!!

How often do we worship the gift instead of the Giver? *I want to scream, SERIOUSLY?! The only wood that needs knocking on is between your EARS!!*

If the tornado missed you, thank God! If you made it through without getting into a wreck, thank God!! If the storm blew out to sea, THANK GOD!!

Let's go one step further...if the tornado took your house and turned it into a million toothpicks, thank God!! He will provide you another. If the wreck put you in the hospital, thank God! He is right there with you every step of the way. If the storm came and settled over the top of your umbrella, stand strong and thank God!! His umbrella is big enough for the both of you!! Worship the Giver.

Lesson 18

Me, Only Different

Though it was just for a short time, being disabled changed me in a lot of ways. Besides giving me a new understanding and compassion for people, I realized some things about myself. I thought I had lost so many things that were important to me when I couldn't walk – the ability to dance and sing. I really thought I couldn't worship if I couldn't stand. What I realized was that I had only lost the ability to choose what and how I did things. Now don't get me wrong – that's huge! But I **was** able to dance. I **was** able to sing. I **was** able to worship. I just did those things sitting down. And God was responding to my heart when I worshipped, not whether I could stand or not.

Family became everything to me. Protecting our home, our kids, and our time together became my number one priority. I will never regret those early years I spent with the children, irreplaceable and unforgettable years. Precious memories that still go with me each day. I learned the importance of family. My parents had demonstrated this to me growing up but through the disability, I learned it firsthand.

About a year after my healing, I was driving down the road one day listening to my favorite Christian radio station when a song began to play. A familiar song. THE song. As it began to play…*hmm hmm hmm hmm*

hmm, hmm hmm hmm hmm… and I heard the words, I began to cry. *Change my heart Oh God. Make it ever true. Change my heart Oh God. Make me more like You.*

Never having heard the words before, I had no idea that the whole time we were in the hospital humming this song, the words were asking God to change my heart! I couldn't believe it. I got my mom on the phone. *"Mom, you have to hear this!"* I cranked up the radio and put the phone to the speaker – *Do you hear this?* Mom began to cry too. We asked Him to change our hearts. And He did.

I wouldn't say everything that changed in me was good. It became very important to me that no one knew that I still had any weak areas physically. I began working at our church, helping one of the pastors. Within a few months, I was the church administrator and had my hand in almost every pot. Only the senior pastor and one other staff member knew when I was hired that I still had numbness in my feet and legs and could not climb stairs. It was very important to me that no one knew because I didn't want anyone to think of me as "handicapped." Yes, very clearly pride and ego.

This began what would turn into years of a workaholic mentality. I had to do more, be more, accomplish more than anyone else. It would take years for God to break that off of me.

A couple of years after my healing, I was coming out of my office at the church when a friend of mine met me in the hallway, tears in her eyes. I asked her what was wrong and she said, *"I just realized who you are!"* I immediately thought she must have met my very popular pastor-father. So, I smiled and said, *"Who?"* She looked at me so seriously and said, *"You're the lady in the wheelchair!"*

Wow! In that moment God reminded me of all He had done for me. I realized that God healed my body not just for me. My healing was also for others who needed to experience God's power, others who needed a reminder of who God is and what He's able to do. A lifelong boost of faith!

I didn't know that day how much I would need that boost of faith in the years to come. Many more storms would blow my way. That's another story…

Lesson 18: Was it Worth it?

Many time I've been asked that question. *Was it worth it?* Yes, it most definitely was worth it. *Would I want to repeat it?* Of course not. If I could just wake up on April 28, 1999, knowing then what I know now and NOT have to experience it all, SURE I would vote to skip the next 6 months. For better or for worse, that's not the way it works.

God knows each of us well enough to know what it takes to mold and make us into the type of vessel He can use. Jeremiah shared an example of a man going to the house of a potter. (Jeremiah 18:1-6) The potter was working on the wheel making a pot but the pot was marred. So the potter reshaped it into another pot. The scripture says *"as it seemed best to him."* God states in verses 5-6 *"Can*

I not do with you as the potter does? Like clay in the hand of the potter so you are in my hand."

God shapes us and molds us into what He intended us to be. Only then can we be an example of Jesus to others. Be able to bless others and walk in such a way that others will see Him and want to know Him as we do.

Is it painful sometimes to be shaped and molded by God? You bet it is!!

Is it worth it when you realize one day you have a changed heart? **Absolutely!!**

Lesson 19

The Days That Followed

The days and months after my healing were not all smooth sailing. I became a workaholic. I found immense pleasure in knowing that I was able to "do all things" again. I enjoyed being the helper instead of the one that needed help. I found I had something to "prove" now. Not to anyone in particular but more to myself. I really wasn't sure for quite some time whether I should talk about my healing or keep it to myself.

I know that may sound strange, but a LOT of people didn't believe me. I would hear it in their questions. See it in the looks they exchanged. If they were not one of the few to have witnessed it, they truly had a hard time believing it. Not everyone, but more than I expected.

My physician was speechless. *"Never seen anything like it."* Social Security wanted the disability money back that they had given me while I was disabled. *Yes, that's still ongoing.* Even some people I went to church with often seemed skeptical.

After a while, I realized I really didn't care what others thought. I had lived it. I KNEW what had happened. So, I told people about it every chance I got!!

I'm sure you're thinking I must be this mighty woman of faith now. I guess in some ways I am, but I have not walked every step that way. Over the next 15 years, I faced drugs, pornography and alcohol addictions in my family. All sorts of job and financial challenges came our way. My marriage would be torn apart and I would start my life over as a single lady after 26 years.

Did I walk strong and steadfast in faith every step of it? No. Many, many times I was face down on my floor, crying my eyes out. Praying that God would take me Home. Unable to face another moment of the day. Wailing to anyone who would listen. Pretty pathetic really.

But I found that in the worst moments of my life, God was the closest to me. Or maybe I drew the closest to Him. ☺ Regardless, He was there. Every moment of every day. The good, the bad AND the ugly!

Again, I found myself so many times filled with fear. No longer was it fear about whether I would lose my smile. Now I feared losing my child. My husband. Life as I knew it.

And in my worst fears, again God was there. In my darkest moments, just like in that hospital, He was with me. Cradling me in His arms, reminding me He was there. Reminding me that He loved my family even more than I did. I just needed to trust Him to work it all out.

Lesson 19: Who Can I Trust?

Ever been lied to? Ever been betrayed? Sure, if you've taken more than two breaths, somebody has betrayed you. At birth, that new baby boy thinks he's getting mama's milk until some nurse shoves a glycerin-filled bottle in his mouth. *Betrayed!!* ☺

If only they were ALL that simple, right?

So, what do you do when you realize trust has been broken by the ones closest to you? A friend? Your spouse? Your kids? Your parents? Your boss? The list could go on and on, right?

Truth is we were never meant to put our trust in people. We were created to trust God. Over and over in the Bible, we are told to put our trust in God. David tells us throughout the book of Psalms (37:3; 40:4; 118:8-9; 125:1) to trust in God. Isaiah told us several times (12:2; 5:10) to not fear but trust in the Lord. Jeremiah speaks of trusting God and not men.

How do I know I can trust God? That's easy! If you've trusted God before, you will know He has never let you down. He is *always* faithful. Never betrays our trust.

If you've never trusted Him before, put Him to the test. Trust Him now. Let Him prove He is true to His word. He will be faithful to you like no other.

Lord, help me to trust You with the deepest, most important parts of my life.

Lesson 20

Girl, What's Going On?

Do you ever feel like you have two sides to your personality? I don't mean a "split personality" but rather, two sides to your spiritual personality.

One minute you're walking along solid in your faith, speaking it, walking it, living it. Then, in a flash, out comes the Noodle. The side that falls limp at the slightest test. The words are now full of doubt, or worse death. The actions are scattered and unfocused. You have now officially fallen back to that spineless, jellyfish person who seems to have no faith at all.

It's so easy to judge others harshly when you're having a Super Faith Day!! You hear someone "whining" about their life and think, *"Where's HER faith? I thought she was a CHRISTIAN!!"*

Have I done that?

Well, of course not!! This book is for YOU!!

Honestly, of course, I have. Sad. After that whole long process to give me a changed heart, I actually find myself falling back into that egotistical, judgmental girl sometimes. Or worse....

The Noodle!

How in the world could I be a Noodle in my faith?

It's hard to imagine how a person who has experienced SO much faith could ever be a spineless, jellyfish in her faith – but I have! And when you're hanging limp in your faith, it's SO easy to make excuses for yourself. *You just don't understand....* We can actually begin to think that God doesn't even understand.

In some of those toughest moments, I found myself asking God why, how, what, when, IF...

Why *did this happen, God?*

HOW *are you going to fix it?*

What should **I** *do?*

WHEN *are you going to do something??*

IF *it ever gets right....*

Even as I write this, I'm amazed that God hasn't just snuffed me out with a lightning bolt or something!! I can hear Him responding to Job when Job wailed and lashed out about all he went through (and Job went through some STUFF)....

Job, did YOU hang the stars in place?
Did YOU cause the sun to rise or set today?

And God goes on and ON, letting Job know that He, God, is in control of EVERYTHING. I wonder sometimes if God doesn't want to yell in frustration, *"Girl, what's going on?"* Where is my faith? Why do I pick back up things from the past?

Lesson 20: Drag It or Leave It?

How easy it is to fall back into those old flesh patterns! Our bad habits. Our addictions. Speaking words that tear down ourselves and others. Bringing the enemy into our homes, our bodies, our relationships.

God has given each of us an opportunity to walk in new life. To leave the past behind and walk free of it once and for all. Does that mean we will never be tempted or tested? Absolutely not. It means we will no longer be CONTROLLED by those things of the past. We can walk free IF we walk in the power we have through Jesus Christ. (Romans 6:18, 22) OR we can be like that dog and return to our sin (Proverbs 26:11).

Jesus paid the ultimate price for our sins so that we would not have to. Hebrews 9:26 says He "put away sin" through His sacrifice. *Why then Lord, do I pick it back up?*

I pray that today, Lord, I will stop dragging my sin behind me, making excuses for it, protecting it, shielding it from the Light. I pray Lord that You will shine Your Light of righteousness upon me and my sin, expose it, reveal it, put it behind me once and for all. Your sacrifice was enough for me, Lord.

Lesson 21

A Changed Heart

Am I really different? Or is this all just words on paper?

I can honestly say I am not the same person since Guillain-Barre entered my life. Does that mean I have "arrived" spiritually? Well, you already know the answer to that – definitely NOT! But when He took me through this process and changed my heart, He taught me a LOT of things. Some I learned TOTALLY. And some I'm still learning.

I learned that God is ALWAYS faithful. I'm still learning to turn to Him first before anything or anyone.

I learned that God is ALWAYS here with me. I'm still learning that I'm going to be just fine even if it's just Him and me.

I learned that God loves my children MORE than me. I'm still learning to be silent in their lives and let Him show them His love for them.

I learned that God is in TOTAL control and doesn't need my help. I'm still learning to sit still when He tells me to wait and pray.

God is so faithful, to the lady in the wheelchair so many years ago, to the lady He carried through major storms, and to each of us that turn to Him. My God is no respecter of persons, which means what He has done for me, He will do for you. He is here for you. He loves you. Turn to Him and let Him carry you through this life. He is faithful.

Lord, the lady in the wheelchair thanks you. Thank You Lord for carrying me through Guillain-Barre and the storms that followed. Thank You for healing my body and most importantly, thank You Lord for changing my heart.

Lesson 21: God Wants to Change <u>Every</u> Heart

Each one of us needs a changed heart. The one we came with is wounded and hurt. Full of doubts, fears and flesh. God wants to create in us a clean heart. In my life, God has needed to change my heart again and again. I think it's like peeling an onion. It would be nice if He could do it all in one step but my "flesh" won't let Him. I tend to justify and want to hang onto some of my sin patterns. So, He peels it away layer by layer, giving me a new heart.

So, how do we get that peeling away to a fresh, clean heart? Some readers may have never known this God I write about; while others may have known Him for years. I believe we can follow the same steps each time.

First, we need to thank Him for His faithfulness and for providing a sacrifice for us through Jesus' death on the cross. *Lord, I thank you for loving me before I even knew You. I thank You for allowing Jesus to die for me on the*

cross so that my sins could be forgiven. Jesus, I thank you for sacrificing yourself for me.
Second, we can ask Him to give us a new heart. *Lord, create in me a new clean heart. Strip away those things that don't need to be there. Put them behind me once and for all. Make for me a new heart, filled with all those things that I need to have to be more like You.*

Finally, we must trust Him with our daily lives. *Lord, I need You to be first in my life. I want to be able to trust You completely with my life. Help me, Lord, to depend on You totally. Help me to turn to You each day, in every situation, and follow what You tell me to do. Thank you Lord for making me a new creation today. In Jesus' Name, Amen.*

Dear Reader,

If you just read the prayer above and realized for the first time in your life you really want Jesus Christ to be number one in your life, please write and let me know. I would love to help you find a Bible-teaching church in your area to get connected with to help you grow strong in your relationship with the Lord. My email address is prazhzname@yahoo.com.

Yes, that's "Praise His Name". ☺ Blessings, Tami L. Sanders

NOTE TO THE READER

Sharing the message of Christ's love through word and song has been a lifelong emphasis for Tami Sanders. Having served in ministry for most of her life, Tami continues to seek opportunities to tell others about God's power, His grace and His love for them. Tami lives in the beautiful mountains of North Carolina near her children and their families. She still believes in miracles and walks daily in the knowledge of God's ability to accomplish the impossible!

Tami would love to come and encourage your church or group in believing for the impossible through prayer. To receive information about hosting an event with Tami, please go to our web site, www.prazhznameministries.com.

The Lady in the Wheelchair

Made in the USA
Charleston, SC
12 February 2017